pasta sauces

simple and delicious easy-to-make recipes

Christine McFadden

This is a Parragon Publishing Book

This edition published in 2004

Parragon Publishing
Queen Street House
4 Queen Street
Bath, BA1 1HE, UK

ISBN: 1-40543-644-1

Printed in China

Produced by
THE BRIDGEWATER BOOK COMPANY LTD

Photographer: Simon Punter
Home Economist: Ricky Turner

Cover Photography: Calvey Taylor-Haw
Home Economist: Ruth Pollock

NOTES FOR THE READER

- This book uses imperial, metric, and cup measurements. Follow the same units of measurement throughout; do not mix imperial and metric.

- All spoon measurements are level: teaspoons are assumed to be 5 ml, and tablespoons are assumed to be 15 ml.

- Unless otherwise stated, milk is assumed to be whole milk, eggs and individual vegetables such as potatoes are medium, and pepper is freshly ground black pepper.

- Recipes using raw or very lightly cooked eggs should be avoided by infants, the elderly, pregnant women, convalescents, and anyone suffering from an illness.

- The times given are an approximate guide only. Preparation times differ according to the techniques used by different people and the cooking times may also vary from those given. Optional ingredients, variations, or serving suggestions have not been included in the calculations.

contents

introduction

Cooked in minutes and easy on the purse, pasta is one of the most versatile of foods, combining happily with a wide variety of sauces. Although meat-based sauces are among the best known, vegetables provide inspiration for many delicious sauces, as do fish and seafood.

Pasta comes in a large number of shapes: flat and round ribbons, tubes, quills, and corkscrews, to name but a few. Each shape lends itself to a particular sauce style. For example, long, thin pasta, such as spaghetti, is best for tomato or oil-based sauces, which coat the surface and cling to it. Wide, flat ribbons, such as fettucine, go well with cream sauces. Shapes or short, hollow tubes are perfect for chunkier sauces because they trap tasty morsels in their crevices.

To cook perfect pasta, use a large pan so the pasta has enough room to move around freely. Allow 4 cups of water for every cup of dried pasta (4 oz/115 g).

meat sauce with mushrooms & tomatoes
page 12

asparagus & gorgonzola sauce with cream
page 58

Bring the water to a fast boil, then add the salt and pasta together, stirring once. Cooking time depends on the type of pasta. It is ready when al dente—tender, but still firm to the bite and slightly chewy. Be careful not to overcook. It is generally better to cook the sauce before the pasta; sauces can be kept waiting, but pasta cannot—it becomes sticky!

Key to Recipes

easy

Recipes are graded as follows:
1 spoon = easy;
2 spoons = very easy;
3 spoons = extremely easy.

serves 4

Recipes generally serve four people. Simply halve the ingredients to serve two, taking care not to mix metric and imperial measurements.

15 minutes

Preparation time. Where marinating or soaking are involved, these times have been added on separately: eg, 15 minutes + 30 minutes to marinate.

40 minutes

Cooking time. Cooking times do not include the cooking of side dishes or accompaniments served with the main dishes.

shrimp & garlic sauce with cream
page 78

tuna with garlic, lemon, capers & olives
page 86

Rich, hearty, meat-based sauces include the universally popular Bolognese, which needs no introduction. There are also irresistible sauces made with coarse-cut sausages or bacon and enriched with tomatoes, mushrooms, or bell peppers. Less well-known are more delicate sauces made with chicken. These often include generous amounts of cream and freshly grated cheese for richness and flavor. All the sauces are simple to prepare and are equally suitable for relaxed entertaining or family suppers.

meat & poultry sauces

classic bolognese meat sauce

very easy   serves 4

15 minutes   1 hour 15 minutes

ingredients

2 tbsp olive oil
1 tbsp butter
1 small onion, chopped finely
1 carrot, chopped finely
1 celery stalk, chopped finely
1 cup mushrooms, diced
2 cups ground beef
¼ cup unsmoked bacon
   or ham, diced
2 chicken livers, chopped
2 tbsp tomato paste

½ cup dry white wine
salt and pepper
½ tsp freshly grated nutmeg
1¼ cups chicken bouillon
½ cup heavy cream
1 lb/450 g dried spaghetti

2 tbsp chopped fresh parsley,
   to garnish

freshly grated Parmesan cheese, to serve

Heat the oil and butter in a large pan over a medium heat. Add the onion, carrot, celery, and mushrooms to the pan, then cook until soft. Add the beef and bacon to the pan and cook until the beef is evenly browned.

Stir in the chicken livers and tomato paste and cook for 2–3 minutes. Pour in the wine and season with salt, pepper, and the nutmeg. Add the bouillon. Bring to a boil, then cover and simmer gently over a low heat for 1 hour. Stir in the cream and simmer, uncovered, until reduced.

Cook the pasta in plenty of boiling salted water until al dente. Drain and transfer to a warm serving dish.

Pour half the sauce over the pasta. Toss well to mix. Spoon the remaining sauce over the top.

Garnish with the parsley and serve at once with Parmesan cheese.

macaroni with sausage, pepperoncini & olives

very easy   serves 4

10–15 minutes   15 minutes

ingredients

1 tbsp olive oil

1 large onion, chopped finely

2 garlic cloves, chopped very finely

2 cups pork sausage, peeled and chopped coarsely

3 canned pepperoncini, or other hot red peppers, drained and sliced

14 oz/400 g canned chopped tomatoes

2 tsp dried oregano

½ cup chicken bouillon or red wine

salt and pepper

4 cups dried macaroni

12–15 black olives, pitted and cut into fourths

⅔ cup freshly grated cheese, such as Cheddar or Gruyère

Heat the oil in a large skillet over a medium heat. Add the onion and cook for 5 minutes until soft. Add the garlic and cook for a few seconds, until just beginning to color. Add the sausage and cook until evenly browned.

Stir in the pepperoncini, tomatoes, oregano, and bouillon. Season with salt and pepper. Bring to a boil, then simmer over a medium heat for 10 minutes, stirring occasionally.

Cook the macaroni in plenty of boiling salted water until al dente. Drain and transfer to a warm serving dish.

Add the olives and half the cheese to the sauce, then stir until the cheese has melted.

Pour the sauce over the pasta. Toss well to mix. Sprinkle with the remaining cheese and serve at once.

meat sauce with mushrooms & tomatoes

very easy   serves 4

10–15 minutes   40 minutes

ingredients

3 tbsp olive oil

4 cups ground beef

4 cups mushrooms, sliced thinly

4 scallions, sliced thinly

4 garlic cloves, chopped very finely

14 oz/400 g canned chopped tomatoes

4 tbsp tomato paste

2 tsp dried oregano

salt and pepper

½ cup bouillon or water

4 cups fresh gnocchi or
    dried conchiglie

freshly grated Parmesan cheese, to serve

Heat 1 tablespoon of the oil in a large skillet over a medium heat. Add the beef and cook until lightly browned. Remove from the skillet and set aside.

Add the rest of the oil to the skillet and cook the mushrooms until softened. Stir in the onions and garlic, then cook for 2 minutes.

Tip the meat back into the skillet and stir in the tomatoes, tomato paste, oregano, salt, pepper, and bouillon. Bring the mixture to a boil, then reduce the heat and simmer over a medium-low heat for 30 minutes.

If serving with gnocchi, bring a pan of lightly salted water to a boil, drop in the gnocchi, return to a boil and drain as soon as they come to the surface. If serving with conchiglie, cook the pasta in plenty of boiling salted water until al dente. Drain and transfer to a warm serving dish.

Pour the sauce over the gnocchi or pasta and toss well to mix. Serve at once with freshly grated Parmesan.

sausage & beef sauce with bell peppers & tomatoes

very easy   serves 4

15–20 minutes   1 hour 15 minutes

2 tbsp olive oil
4 bacon strips, chopped
1 onion, chopped finely
1 green bell pepper, seeded and
   chopped finely
1 cup mushrooms, sliced thinly
4 garlic cloves, sliced thinly
2 cups ground beef
1 cup coarse pork sausage, peeled and
   chopped

1 lb 12 oz/800 g canned chopped tomatoes
1 fresh bay leaf
6 tbsp tomato paste
4 tbsp red wine or bouillon
salt and pepper
4 cups dried penne or rigatoni

freshly grated Parmesan, to serve

Heat the oil in a large skillet over a medium heat. Add the bacon and cook until lightly browned. Add the onion, green bell pepper, mushrooms and garlic. Gently cook for 5–7 minutes until soft.

Stir in the beef and sausage, then cook until browned. Add the tomatoes and bay leaf. Bring to a boil, then simmer over a medium–low heat for 1 hour. Stir in the tomato paste and wine. Season with salt and pepper. Simmer for a few minutes more.

Cook the pasta in plenty of boiling salted water until al dente. Drain and transfer to a warm serving dish.

Pour the sauce over the pasta and toss well to mix. Serve with Parmesan.

chicken & onion cream sauce

very easy   serves 4

10 minutes   35 minutes

ingredients

1 tbsp olive oil

2 tbsp butter

1 garlic clove, chopped very finely

4 boneless, skinless chicken breasts

salt and pepper

1 onion, chopped finely

1 chicken bouillon cube, crumbled

½ cup water

1¼ cups heavy cream

¾ cup milk

6 scallions, green part included,
  sliced diagonally

scant ⅓ cup freshly grated Parmesan cheese

1 lb/450 g dried fettuccine

sprig of fresh flatleaf parsley,
  to garnish

Heat the oil and butter with the garlic in a large skillet over a medium–low heat. Cook the garlic until just beginning to color. Add the chicken breasts and raise the heat to medium. Cook for 4–5 minutes on each side, or until the juices are no longer pink. Season with salt and pepper. Remove from the heat. Remove the chicken breasts, leaving the oil in the skillet. Slice the breasts diagonally into thin strips and set aside.

Reheat the oil in the skillet. Add the onion and gently cook for 5 minutes, or until soft. Add the crumbled bouillon cube and the water. Bring to a boil, then simmer over a medium–low heat for 10 minutes. Stir in the cream, milk, scallions and Parmesan. Simmer until heated through and slightly thickened.

Cook the fettucine in boiling salted water until al dente. Drain and transfer to a warm serving dish. Layer the chicken slices over the pasta. Pour on the sauce, garnish with parsley, and serve at once.

cannelloni with chicken, ricotta & herbs

easy   serves 4

15–20 minutes + 30 minutes to marinate   1 hour

MARINADE
½ cup white wine vinegar
1 garlic clove, crushed
1 cup olive oil

2 tbsp olive oil
4 boneless, skinless chicken
  breasts, diced
6 tbsp butter
generous 2 cups heavy cream
1 tsp salt

1 tsp freshly ground black pepper
¼ tsp freshly grated nutmeg
½ cup freshly grated Parmesan cheese
2 cups ricotta cheese
1 egg, lightly beaten
1 tbsp chopped fresh oregano
2 tbsp chopped fresh basil
8 oz/225 g dried cannelloni
⅔ cup freshly grated mozzarella cheese

sprig of basil, to garnish

In a bowl, combine the vinegar, garlic, and olive oil for the marinade. Add the chicken and marinate for 30 minutes.

Heat 2 tablespoons of olive oil in a skillet. Drain the chicken and cook 5–7 minutes, stirring, until no longer pink. Set aside.

Melt the butter in a pan over a medium–high heat. Add the cream, salt, pepper, and nutmeg. Stir until thickened. Reduce the heat, then add the Parmesan and stir until melted. Remove from the heat.

Heat the oven to 350°F/180°C. In a large bowl, mix together the ricotta, egg, and herbs. Stir in the chicken. Stuff the cannelloni with the chicken mixture. Pour half the sauce into a 9 x 13-inch/23 x 33-cm baking dish. Place the stuffed cannelloni on top. Pour over the remaining sauce. Sprinkle with the mozzarella and cover with aluminum foil. Bake for 45 minutes. Let the dish stand for 10 minutes before serving with basil.

creamy chicken & shiitake sauce

very easy   serves 4

10 minutes   35 minutes
+ 30 minutes
soaking time

ingredients

1⅓ cups dried shiitake mushrooms

1½ cups hot water

1 tbsp olive oil

6 bacon strips, chopped

3 boneless, skinless chicken breasts,
   sliced into strips

2 cups fresh shiitake mushrooms,
   sliced

1 small onion, chopped finely

1 tsp fresh oregano or marjoram,
   chopped finely

generous 1 cup chicken bouillon

1¼ cups whipping cream

salt and pepper

1 lb/450 g dried tagliatelle

½ cup freshly grated Parmesan cheese

sprig of fresh flatleaf parsley, to garnish

Put the dried mushrooms in a bowl with the hot water. Let soak for 30 minutes, or until softened. Remove, squeezing excess water back into the bowl. Strain the liquid in a fine-meshed strainer and reserve. Slice the soaked mushrooms, discarding the stems.

Heat the oil in a large skillet over a medium heat. Add the bacon and chicken, then stir-fry for about 3 minutes. Add the dried and fresh mushrooms, the onion, and oregano. Stir-fry for 5–7 minutes, until soft. Pour in the bouillon and the mushroom liquid. Bring to a boil, stirring. Simmer briskly for about 10 minutes, continuing to stir, until reduced. Add the cream and simmer for 5 minutes, stirring, until beginning to thicken. Season with salt and pepper. Remove the skillet from the heat and set aside.

Cook the pasta until al dente. Drain and transfer to a serving dish. Pour the sauce over the pasta. Add half the Parmesan and mix. Garnish with parsley and serve at once with the remaining Parmesan.

farfalle with chicken, broccoli & roasted red bell peppers

very easy   serves 4

15 minutes   15 minutes

ingredients

4 tbsp olive oil

5 tbsp butter

3 garlic cloves, chopped very finely

1 lb/450 g boneless, skinless chicken
  breasts, diced

¼ tsp dried chili flakes

salt and pepper

1 lb/450 g small broccoli florets

2⅔ cups dried farfalle or fusilli

6 oz/175 g bottled roasted red bell peppers,
  drained and diced

generous 1 cup chicken bouillon

freshly grated Parmesan cheese, to serve

Bring a large pan of salted water to a boil. Meanwhile, heat the olive oil, butter, and garlic in a large skillet over a medium-low heat. Cook the garlic until just beginning to color.

Add the diced chicken, raise the heat to medium and stir-fry for 4–5 minutes, until the chicken is no longer pink. Add the chili flakes and season with salt and pepper. Remove from the heat.

Plunge the broccoli into the boiling water and cook for 2 minutes, until tender-crisp. Remove with a perforated spoon and set aside. Bring the water back to a boil. Add the pasta and cook until al dente. Drain and add to the chicken mixture in the pan. Add the broccoli and roasted bell peppers. Pour in the bouillon. Simmer briskly over a medium-high heat, stirring frequently, until most of the liquid has been absorbed.

Sprinkle with the Parmesan and serve at once.

chicken with basil & pine nut pesto

very easy   serves 4

10 minutes   15 minutes

ingredients

PESTO

1⅔ cups shredded fresh basil

4 fl oz/125 ml extra-virgin olive oil

3 tbsp pine nuts

3 garlic cloves, crushed

salt

½ cup freshly grated Parmesan cheese

2 tbsp freshly grated romano cheese

2 tbsp vegetable oil

4 boneless, skinless chicken breasts

12 oz/350 g dried fettuccine

freshly ground pepper, to taste

sprig of fresh basil, to garnish

To make the pesto, put the basil, olive oil, pine nuts, garlic, and a generous pinch of salt in a food processor or blender. Purée the ingredients until smooth. Scrape the mixture into a bowl and stir in the cheeses.

Heat the vegetable oil in a skillet over a medium heat. Cook the chicken breasts, turning once, for 8–10 minutes, until the juices are no longer pink. Cut into small cubes.

Cook the pasta in plenty of boiling salted water until al dente. Drain and transfer to a warm serving dish. Add the chicken and pesto, then season with pepper. Toss well to mix.

Garnish with a sprig of basil and serve warm.

noodles with chicken satay sauce

very easy

serves 4

10 minutes   20 minutes

ingredients

2 tbsp vegetable oil
1 lb/450 g boneless, skinless
  chicken breasts, cubed
1 red bell pepper, seeded and sliced
4 scallions, green part included,
  sliced diagonally

8 oz/225 g dried vermicelli
  or spaghettini
generous ½ cup smooth peanut butter
1 tsp grated fresh gingerroot
2 tbsp soy sauce
½ cup chicken bouillon

Heat the oil in a large skillet over a medium heat. Add the chicken and cook for 5–7 minutes, until no longer pink. Add the bell pepper and scallions. Cook for 3 minutes, until just soft. Remove from the heat.

Cook the pasta in plenty of boiling salted water until al dente. Drain and return to the pan.

Put the peanut butter, ginger, soy sauce, and chicken bouillon in a large pan. Simmer over a medium-low heat, stirring, until bubbling. Add the cooked vegetables, chicken, and pasta to the peanut mixture. Toss gently until coated with the sauce.

Transfer to a warm serving dish and serve at once.

fusilli with bacon, eggs & mushrooms

very easy   serves 4

10 minutes   15 minutes

ingredients

1 tbsp olive oil

4 strips lean bacon or pancetta

2 cups mushrooms, sliced

2 cups fusilli or conchiglie

salt and pepper

2 eggs, beaten

115 g/4 oz Cheddar or mozzarella cheese, cubed

chopped fresh flatleaf parsley, to garnish

Heat the oil in a skillet over a medium heat. Add the bacon and cook until crisp. Remove with tongs, leaving the drippings in the skillet. Cut into small pieces and keep warm.

Cook the mushrooms in the bacon drippings for 5–7 minutes, until soft. Remove from the heat.

Cook the pasta in plenty of boiling salted water until al dente. Drain and return to the skillet.

Stir the mushrooms, beaten eggs, and the cheese cubes into the pasta. Season with pepper and toss until the eggs have coated the pasta and the cheese has melted.

Transfer to a warm serving dish. Sprinkle with the bacon pieces and parsley and serve at once.

rigatoni with spicy bacon & tomato sauce

very easy

serves 4

10 minutes   45 minutes

ingredients

6 tbsp olive oil
3 garlic cloves, sliced thinly
scant ⅓ cup lean bacon, chopped
1 lb 12 oz/800 g canned
  chopped tomatoes

½ tsp dried chili flakes
salt and pepper
4 cups rigatoni
10 fresh basil leaves, shredded
2 tbsp freshly grated romano cheese

Heat the oil and garlic in a large skillet over a medium-low heat. Cook until the garlic is just beginning to color. Add the bacon and cook until browned.

Stir in the tomatoes and chili flakes. Season with a little salt and pepper. Bring to a boil, then simmer over a medium-low heat for 30–40 minutes, until the oil separates from the tomatoes.

Cook the pasta in plenty of boiling salted water until al dente. Drain and transfer to a warm serving dish.

Pour the sauce over the pasta. Add the basil and romano, then toss well to mix. Serve at once.

ham, tomato & chili sauce

very easy　　serves 4

10–15
minutes　　1 hour

ingredients

1 tbsp olive oil
2 tbsp butter
1 onion, chopped finely
scant ⅔ cup ham, diced
2 garlic cloves, chopped very finely
1 fresh red chili, seeded and
　chopped finely

1 lb 12 oz/800 g canned
　chopped tomatoes
salt and pepper
4 cups bucatini or penne
2 tbsp chopped fresh
　flatleaf parsley
6 tbsp freshly grated Parmesan cheese

Put the olive oil and 1 tablespoon of the butter in a large skillet over a medium-low heat. Add the onion and cook for 10 minutes, until soft and golden. Add the ham and cook for 5 minutes, until lightly browned. Stir in the garlic, chili, and tomatoes. Season with a little salt and pepper. Bring to a boil, then simmer over a medium-low heat for 30–40 minutes, until thickened.

Cook the pasta in plenty of boiling salted water until al dente. Drain and transfer to a warm serving dish.

Pour the sauce over the pasta. Add the parsley, Parmesan, and the remaining butter. Toss well to mix. Serve at once.

spaghetti alla carbonara

very easy   serves 4

10–15
minutes   15 minutes

ingredients

2 tbsp olive oil

1 tbsp butter

⅔ cup lean, smoked bacon, sliced
    into thin strips

3 eggs, lightly beaten

¼ cup freshly grated Parmesan cheese

scant ¼ cup freshly grated romano cheese

1 tbsp chopped fresh flatleaf parsley

4 tbsp light cream

pepper

1 lb/450 g dried spaghetti

Heat the oil and butter in a skillet over a medium-high heat. Add the bacon and cook for 4–5 minutes, until browned. Remove from the heat. Combine the eggs, cheeses, parsley, and cream in a bowl, mixing well. Season with pepper.

Cook the pasta in plenty of boiling salted water until al dente. Drain and return to the skillet.

Quickly add the egg mixture to the pasta, tossing rapidly so that the egg cooks in the heat. Transfer to a warm serving dish.

Briefly reheat the bacon over a high heat. Add to the pasta, toss again and serve at once.

With their flamboyant colors and fresh flavors, Mediterranean-style vegetables and herbs are perfect for pasta sauces. These are among the quickest and easiest sauces to prepare, ranging from the simple concoctions of chopped raw tomatoes, olive oil, and basil to more complex mixtures of roasted bell peppers and garlic, or asparagus and Gorgonzola. Pantry ingredients are put to good use: jars of artichokes, bell peppers, sun-dried tomatoes, and olives all contribute robust flavors that will please vegetarians and meat-eaters alike.

vegetable sauces

sun-dried tomato & goat cheese sauce

very easy   serves 4

10 minutes   10–15
minutes

1 tbsp butter
2 garlic cloves, sliced thinly
8 oz/225 g goat cheese, crumbled
1¼ cups milk
½ cup heavy cream
20 oil-cured sun-dried tomato halves
   (in oil), chopped coarsely

salt and pepper
4 cups dried penne
scant ⅓ cup freshly grated
   Parmesan cheese
10 fresh basil leaves, shredded

Heat the butter and garlic in a skillet over a medium-low heat. Cook until the garlic is just beginning to color. Add the cheese and milk. Stir until the cheese has melted and formed a thick sauce.

Add the cream and sun-dried tomatoes. Cook for about 5 minutes, stirring frequently, until reduced by one-third. Season with salt and pepper. Remove from the heat.

Cook the pasta in plenty of boiling salted water until al dente. Transfer to a warm serving dish.

Briefly reheat the sauce over a low heat. Pour over the pasta. Add the Parmesan and basil, then toss well to mix. Serve at once.

sun-dried tomato sauce with herbs

very easy   serves 4

10–15   20–25
minutes   minutes

ingredients

3 oz/85 g sun-dried tomatoes (not in oil)

3 cups boiling water

2 tbsp olive oil

1 onion, chopped finely

2 large garlic cloves, sliced finely

2 tbsp chopped fresh flatleaf parsley

2 tsp chopped fresh oregano

1 tsp chopped fresh rosemary

salt and pepper

3 cups dried fusilli

10 fresh basil leaves, shredded

3 tbsp freshly grated Parmesan cheese

Put the tomatoes and boiling water in a bowl and let stand for 5 minutes. Using a perforated spoon, remove one-third of the tomatoes from the bowl. Cut into bite-size pieces. Put the remaining tomatoes and water into a blender and purée.

Heat the oil in a large skillet over a medium heat. Add the onion and gently cook for 5 minutes, or until soft. Add the garlic and cook until just beginning to color. Add the puréed tomato and the reserved tomato pieces to the skillet. Bring to a boil, then simmer over a medium-low heat for 10 minutes. Stir in the herbs and season with salt and pepper. Simmer for 1 minute, then remove from the heat.

Cook the pasta in plenty of boiling salted water until al dente. Drain and transfer to a warm serving dish. Briefly reheat the sauce. Pour over the pasta, then add the basil and toss well to mix. Sprinkle with the Parmesan and serve at once.

tomato-chili sauce
with avocado & cilantro

very easy   serves 4

15 minutes   20 minutes

ingredients

3 tbsp olive oil

4 scallions, green part included,
   sliced finely

1 fresh green chili, seeded and chopped
   very finely

2 garlic cloves, chopped very finely

7 oz/200 g canned chopped tomatoes

salt and pepper

3 cups dried farfalle or conchiglie

2 small avocados, peeled and cubed

juice of ½ lime

6 tbsp chopped fresh cilantro

Heat 1 tablespoon of the oil in a skillet over a medium-low heat. Add the scallions and chili, then cook, stirring constantly, for 3–4 minutes, or until just soft. Add the garlic and cook until just beginning to color.

Stir in the tomatoes. Bring to a boil, then simmer the sauce over a medium heat for 10 minutes, stirring, until thickened. Season with salt and pepper.

Cook the pasta in plenty of boiling salted water until al dente. Drain and transfer to a warm serving dish.

Pour the sauce over the pasta. Add the avocados, lime juice, cilantro and remaining olive oil. Toss well to mix. Serve warm or at room temperature.

bell pepper & goat cheese sauce

very easy   serves 4

10 minutes   30 minutes

ingredients

2 tbsp olive oil

1 tbsp butter

1 small onion, chopped finely

4 bell peppers, yellow and red, seeded
   and cut into ¾-inch/2-cm squares

3 garlic cloves, sliced thinly

salt and pepper

4 cups dried rigatoni or penne

4½ oz/125 g goat cheese, crumbled

15 fresh basil leaves, shredded

10 black olives, pitted and sliced

Heat the oil and butter in a large skillet over a medium heat. Add the onion and
cook until soft. Raise the heat to medium-high and add the bell peppers and garlic.
Cook for 12–15 minutes, stirring, until the peppers are tender but not mushy.
Season with salt and pepper. Remove from the heat.

Cook the pasta in plenty of boiling salted water until al dente. Drain and transfer
to a warm serving dish. Add the goat cheese and toss to mix.

Briefly reheat the sauce. Add the basil and olives. Pour over the pasta and toss
well to mix. Serve at once.

tomato sauce with garlic & basil

very easy   serves 4

10 minutes   30 minutes

ingredients

5 tbsp extra-virgin olive oil

1 onion, chopped finely

1 lb 12 oz/800 g canned
chopped tomatoes

4 garlic cloves, cut into fourths

salt and pepper

1 lb/450 g dried spaghetti

large handful fresh basil leaves, shredded

freshly grated Parmesan cheese, to serve

Heat the oil in a large pan over a medium heat. Add the onion and cook gently for 5 minutes, until soft. Add the tomatoes and garlic. Bring to a boil, then simmer over a medium-low heat for 25–30 minutes, or until the oil separates from the tomato. Season with salt and pepper.

Cook the pasta in plenty of boiling salted water until al dente. Drain and transfer to a warm serving dish.

Pour the sauce over the pasta. Add the basil and toss well to mix. Serve at once with Parmesan.

raw tomato sauce with olive oil, garlic & basil

ingredients

extremely
easy

serves 4

10 minutes
+ 30 minutes
standing
time

8–10
minutes

1 lb 4 oz/550 g large, ripe tomatoes,
   peeled, seeded, and diced
½ cup extra-virgin olive oil
4 garlic cloves, chopped very finely

large handful fresh basil leaves, shredded
3 tbsp chopped fresh oregano or marjoram
salt and pepper
4 cups dried conchiglie

Combine the tomatoes, olive oil, garlic, basil, and oregano in a bowl that is large enough to eventually accommodate the cooked pasta. Season generously with salt and pepper. Cover the bowl with plastic wrap and let stand at room temperature for at least 30 minutes.

Cook the pasta in plenty of boiling salted water until al dente. Drain thoroughly and immediately add to the tomatoes.

Toss well to mix. Serve at room temperature.

cherry tomato sauce with olives

very easy   serves 4

10 minutes   30 minutes

ingredients

4 tbsp olive oil

2 lb/900 g cherry tomatoes

2 garlic cloves, chopped very finely

1 tbsp chopped fresh oregano or marjoram

¾ tsp dried chili flakes

20–25 black olives, pitted and sliced

pepper

3 cups dried conchiglie

zest of ½ lemon, grated

scant ¾ cup freshly grated Parmesan cheese

Heat the oil in a large skillet over a medium-high heat. Add the cherry tomatoes and stir until evenly coated with oil. Cover and cook for 10–12 minutes, shaking the skillet and stirring once, until all the tomatoes have split.

Add the garlic, oregano, chili flakes, and olives. Season with pepper. Reduce the heat to low and simmer, uncovered, for another 7–10 minutes.

Cook the pasta in plenty of boiling salted water until al dente. Drain well and transfer to a warm serving dish.

Pour half the sauce over the pasta. Toss well to mix. Spoon the rest of the sauce over the top. Sprinkle with the grated lemon zest and Parmesan and serve at once.

roasted red bell pepper sauce

very easy   serves 4

10 minutes   35 minutes

ingredients

4 red bell peppers, halved and seeded
5 tbsp olive oil
1 small red onion, sliced finely
2 garlic cloves, chopped very finely
2 tbsp chopped fresh flatleaf parsley
1 tsp chopped fresh thyme

salt and pepper
3 cups dried penne or rigatoni

4 tbsp toasted fresh bread crumbs,
   to garnish

freshly grated Parmesan cheese, to serve

Place the bell peppers cut-side down in a roasting pan. Roast in a preheated oven at 425°F/220°C for 15–20 minutes, or until the skin begins to blacken. Let cool slightly. Remove the skin from the bell peppers. Slice the flesh into thin strips.

Heat the oil in a large skillet over a medium heat. Add the onion and cook for 5 minutes, or until soft. Add the garlic and cook until just beginning to color. Stir in the roasted bell pepper strips, parsley, and thyme. Season with salt and pepper. Stir until heated through.

Cook the pasta in plenty of boiling salted water until al dente. Drain well and transfer to a warm serving dish.

Pour the sauce over the pasta and toss well to mix. Sprinkle with the bread crumbs and serve at once with Parmesan.

roasted garlic & red bell pepper sauce

ingredients

very easy   serves 4

10 minutes   30 minutes

6 large garlic cloves, unpeeled
14 oz/400 g bottled roasted red bell
  peppers, drained and sliced
7 oz/200 g canned chopped tomatoes
3 tbsp olive oil
¾ tsp dried chili flakes

1 tsp chopped fresh thyme or oregano
salt and pepper
12 oz/350 g dried spaghetti, bucatini,
  or linguine

freshly grated Parmesan cheese, to serve

Place the unpeeled garlic cloves in a shallow, ovenproof dish. Roast in a preheated oven at 400°F/200°C for 7–10 minutes, until the cloves feel soft.

Put the bell peppers, tomatoes, and oil in a food processor or blender, then purée. Squeeze the garlic flesh into the purée. Add the chili flakes and oregano. Season with salt and pepper. Blend again, then scrape into a pan and set aside.

Cook the pasta in plenty of boiling salted water until al dente. Drain and transfer to a warm serving dish.

Reheat the sauce and pour over the pasta. Toss well to mix. Serve at once with Parmesan.

marinated artichoke sauce
with onions & tomatoes

ingredients

very easy   serves 4

10 minutes   50 minutes

10 oz/280 g marinated artichoke hearts
(in jar)
3 tbsp olive oil
1 onion, chopped finely
3 garlic cloves, chopped very finely
1 tsp dried oregano

¼ tsp dried chili flakes
14 oz/400 g canned chopped tomatoes
salt and pepper
3 cups dried conchiglie
scant ¼ cup freshly grated Parmesan cheese
3 tbsp chopped fresh flatleaf parsley

Drain the artichoke hearts, reserving the marinade. Heat the oil in a large pan over a medium heat. Add the onion and cook for 5 minutes, until translucent. Add the garlic, oregano, chili flakes, and the reserved marinade. Cook for 5 more minutes.

Stir in the tomatoes. Bring to a boil, then simmer over a medium-low heat for 30 minutes. Season generously with salt and pepper.

Cook the pasta in plenty of boiling salted water until al dente. Drain and transfer to a warm serving dish.

Add the artichokes, Parmesan, and parsley to the sauce. Cook for a few minutes until heated through.

Pour the sauce over the pasta. Toss well to mix. Serve at once.

asparagus & gorgonzola sauce
with cream

extremely
easy

serves 4

10 minutes   20 minutes

1 lb/450 g asparagus tips
olive oil
salt and pepper

8 oz/225 g Gorgonzola cheese, crumbled
¾ cup heavy cream
3 cups dried penne

Place the asparagus tips in a single layer in a shallow ovenproof dish.
Sprinkle with a little olive oil. Season with salt and pepper. Turn to coat in the oil
and seasoning.

Roast in a preheated oven at 450°F/230°C for 10–12 minutes, until slightly
browned and just tender. Set aside and keep warm.

Combine the crumbled cheese with the cream in a bowl. Season with salt
and pepper.

Cook the pasta in plenty of boiling salted water until al dente. Drain and transfer
to a warm serving dish.

Immediately add the asparagus and the cheese mixture. Toss well until the cheese
has melted and the pasta is coated with the sauce. Serve at once.

spaghetti with garlic & oil sauce

extremely easy   serves 4

10 minutes   25 minutes

ingredients

1 lb/450 g dried spaghetti
salt
½ cup extra-virgin olive oil

4 garlic cloves, chopped very finely
¼ tsp dried chili flakes
3 tbsp chopped fresh flatleaf parsley

Cook the pasta in plenty of boiling salted water until al dente. Drain and transfer to a warm serving dish. Season with salt to taste and keep the dish warm.

Heat the oil in a small pan over a medium-low heat. Add the garlic and chili flakes. Cook for 1–2 minutes, or until the garlic is just beginning to color. Immediately pour the contents of the pan over the pasta. Toss thoroughly to mix.

Sprinkle with the parsley and toss again. Serve at once.

roasted garlic cream sauce

easy   serves 4

10 minutes   20 minutes

ingredients

2 large heads garlic
2½ cups heavy cream
3 thin strips lemon peel
salt and pepper
12 oz/350 g dried fettuccine or tagliatelle

⅓ cup freshly grated Parmesan cheese

2 tbsp chopped fresh flatleaf parsley,
   to garnish

Separate the garlic cloves, removing as much of the papery skin as possible, but leaving a thin layer intact. Place the cloves in a shallow ovenproof dish. Roast in a preheated oven at 400°F/200°C for 7–10 minutes until the cloves feel soft.

When the garlic is cool enough to handle, remove the skin. Put the cloves in a small pan with the cream and lemon peel. Bring to a boil, then simmer gently over a low heat for about 5 minutes, or until thickened. Push the sauce through a fine-meshed strainer, pressing with the back of a wooden spoon. Return to the pan. Season with salt and pepper and set aside.

Cook the pasta in plenty of boiling salted water until al dente. Drain and transfer to a warm serving dish. Stir the Parmesan into the sauce and reheat gently. Pour the sauce over the pasta and toss well to mix. Sprinkle with the parsley. Serve at once.

mushroom & spinach sauce with feta

very easy   serves 4

15 minutes   20 minutes

ingredients

3 tbsp olive oil

4 cups mushrooms, sliced

2 garlic cloves, chopped very finely

2 tbsp chopped fresh flatleaf parsley

salt and pepper

4 cups dried rigatoni

3 cups trimmed baby spinach, chopped coarsely

1 cup hot chicken bouillon

TO GARNISH

2 oz/55 g feta cheese (drained weight), crumbled

1 tsp chopped fresh thyme

Heat the oil in a large skillet over a medium-high heat. Add the mushrooms and cook for 5 minutes, or until the moisture starts to evaporate. Add the garlic and parsley, then cook for a few seconds more. Season with salt and pepper. Remove the cooking pan from the heat.

Cook the pasta in plenty of boiling salted water until al dente. Drain and immediately return to the pan.

Add the spinach, hot bouillon and the mushrooms to the pasta. Toss well until the spinach has wilted. Transfer to a warm serving dish. Sprinkle with the feta and thyme and serve at once.

zucchini sauce with lemon & rosemary

very easy   serves 4

10 minutes   20 minutes

ingredients

6 tbsp olive oil
1 small onion, sliced very thinly
2 garlic cloves, chopped very finely
2 tbsp chopped fresh rosemary
1 tbsp chopped fresh
   flatleaf parsley

1 lb/450 g small zucchini, cut into
   1½ x ¼-inch/4 cm x 5-mm strips
finely grated peel of 1 lemon
salt and pepper
4 cups fusilli
4 tbsp freshly grated Parmesan cheese

Heat the olive oil in a large skillet over a medium-low heat. Add the onion and gently cook, stirring occasionally, for about 10 minutes, or until golden.

Raise the heat to medium-high. Add the garlic, rosemary, and parsley. Cook for a few seconds, stirring.

Add the zucchini and lemon peel. Cook for 5–7 minutes, stirring occasionally, until the zucchini are just tender. Season with salt and pepper. Remove from the heat.

Cook the pasta in plenty of boiling salted water until al dente. Drain and transfer to a warm serving dish.

Briefly reheat the zucchini. Pour over the pasta and toss well to mix. Sprinkle with the Parmesan and serve at once.

Fish and seafood are ideal candidates for pasta sauces, especially if you stock up with pantry basics such as bottled clams and cans of tuna and anchovies. These need only the briefest of cooking times, letting you get a meal on the table in minutes. Shrimp can be combined with tomatoes, garlic, and chili for a robust Mediterranean sauce, or sizzled Asian-style with ginger and spices, while smoked salmon, mussels, and scallops can form the basis of rich cream or tomato-based sauces that are ideal for entertaining.

fish & seafood sauces

spaghetti with anchovies, olives, capers & tomatoes

very easy   serves 4

10 minutes   35–40 minutes

ingredients

6 tbsp olive oil

4 anchovy fillets, chopped

2 garlic cloves, chopped very finely

1 lb 12 oz/800 g canned chopped tomatoes

1 tsp dried oregano

¼ tsp dried chili flakes

salt and pepper

12 oz/350 g dried spaghetti

10–12 black olives, pitted and sliced

2 tbsp capers, drained

Heat the oil with the anchovies in a large skillet over a low heat. Stir until the anchovies dissolve. Add the garlic and cook for a few seconds, or until just beginning to color. Add the tomatoes, oregano, and chili flakes, then season with salt and pepper. Bring to a boil, then simmer over a medium-low heat for 30 minutes, or until the oil begins to separate from the tomatoes.

Cook the pasta in plenty of boiling salted water until al dente. Drain and transfer to a warm serving dish.

Add the olives and capers to the sauce. Pour over the pasta and toss well to mix. Serve at once.

clam & tomato sauce

very easy   serves 4

10 minutes   35 minutes

ingredients

14 oz/400 g clams or scallops
  in brine (in jar)
4 tbsp olive oil
4 garlic cloves, chopped very finely
1 lb 12 oz/800 g canned
  chopped tomatoes

3 tbsp chopped fresh
  flatleaf parsley
½ tsp dried chili flakes
salt
4 cups dried riccioli or fusilli

Drain the clams or scallops, reserving the liquid from the jar.

Heat the oil and garlic in a large pan over a low heat. Cook the garlic for a few seconds, until just beginning to color. Add the tomatoes, the reserved clam juice, parsley, chili flakes, and a little salt. Bring to a boil, then simmer over a medium-low heat for 30 minutes, until the oil separates from the tomatoes.

Cook the pasta in plenty of boiling salted water until al dente. Drain and transfer to a warm serving dish.

Add the clams to the sauce, stirring until heated through. Pour the sauce over the pasta. Toss well to mix. Serve at once.

shrimp sauce with tomatoes, garlic & chili

very easy   serves 4

10 minutes   35 minutes

ingredients

4 tbsp olive oil
5 garlic cloves, chopped very finely
14 oz/400 g canned chopped tomatoes
1 fresh red chili, seeded and
   chopped very finely

salt and pepper
1 lb/450 g dried linguine or spaghetti
12 oz/350 g raw jumbo shrimp, shelled
2 tbsp chopped fresh flatleaf parsley

Heat 2 tablespoons of the oil and the garlic in a pan over a medium-low heat. Cook the garlic until just beginning to color. Add the tomatoes and chili. Bring to a boil, then simmer over a medium-low heat for 30 minutes, or until the oil separates from the tomatoes. Season with salt and pepper.

Cook the pasta in plenty of boiling salted water until al dente. Drain and return to the pan.

Heat the remaining oil in a skillet over a high heat. Add the shrimp and stir-fry for 2 minutes until pink. Add the shrimp to the tomato mixture. Stir in the parsley. Simmer over a low heat until bubbling.

Transfer the pasta to a warm serving dish. Pour the sauce over the pasta. Toss well to mix and serve at once.

scallop & leek sauce

very easy   serves 4

10 minutes   15 minutes

ingredients

14 oz/400 g scallops or clams in brine
  (in jar)
3 tbsp olive oil
2 large leeks (white part only),
  sliced lengthwise and cut into thin
  2-inch/5-cm strips

2 garlic cloves, chopped very finely
4 tbsp dry white wine
1 bay leaf
salt and pepper
12 oz/350 g dried spaghetti or linguine
3 tbsp fresh flatleaf parsley

Drain the scallops or clams, reserving the liquid from the jar.

Heat the oil in a large skillet over a medium–low heat. Add the leeks and garlic,
then cook gently for 3–4 minutes, or until the leeks are tender-crisp. Stir in the
wine and cook for 1–2 minutes, or until evaporated. Add the bay leaf, scallops, or
clams, and the reserved liquid. Season with salt and pepper. Simmer for 5
minutes, then remove from the heat.

Cook the pasta in plenty of boiling salted water until al dente. Drain and transfer
to a warm serving dish.

Briefly reheat the sauce and pour over the pasta. Add the parsley and toss well
to mix. Serve at once.

shrimp & garlic sauce with cream

very easy   serves 4

15 minutes   15 minutes

ingredients

3 tbsp olive oil

3 tbsp butter

4 garlic cloves, chopped very finely

2 tbsp finely diced red bell pepper

2 tbsp tomato paste

½ cup dry white wine

1 lb/450 g tagliatelle or spaghetti

12 oz/350 g raw shrimp, shelled,
    cut into ½-inch/1-cm pieces

½ cup heavy cream

salt and pepper

3 tbsp chopped fresh flatleaf parsley

Heat the oil and butter in a pan over a medium-low heat. Add the garlic and red bell pepper. Cook for a few seconds, or until the garlic is just beginning to color. Stir in the tomato paste and wine. Cook for 10 minutes, stirring.

Cook the pasta in plenty of boiling salted water until al dente. Drain and return to the pan.

Add the shrimp to the sauce and raise the heat to medium-high. Cook for 2 minutes, stirring, until the shrimp turn pink. Reduce the heat and stir in the cream. Cook for 1 minute, stirring constantly, until thickened. Season with salt and pepper.

Transfer the pasta to a warm serving dish. Pour the sauce over the pasta. Sprinkle with the parsley. Toss well to mix and serve at once.

spicy shrimp sauce with ginger

very easy   serves 4

10 minutes   10 minutes

ingredients

4 tbsp passata (strained tomatoes)

1¼ cups light cream

1½ tsp grated fresh gingerroot

¼ tsp cayenne

1 tbsp lemon juice

1 tsp ground cumin

1 tsp salt

¼ tsp pepper

1 lb/450 g dried flat rice noodles

3 tbsp vegetable oil

3 garlic cloves, chopped very finely

1 lb/450 g raw jumbo shrimp, shelled

2 tbsp chopped fresh cilantro

Combine the passata, cream, ginger, cayenne, lemon juice, cumin, salt, and pepper in a small pan, mixing well. Cook the mixture over a medium heat, stirring, until bubbling, then remove from the heat.

Cook the noodles according to the packet instructions. Drain and transfer to a warm serving dish.

Heat the oil and garlic in a large skillet over a medium-low heat. Cook until the garlic just begins to color. Add the shrimp and raise the heat to medium-high. Stir-fry for 2 minutes, or until the shrimp are pink. Stir in the sauce and 1 tablespoon of the cilantro. Cook for another minute.

Pour the shrimp mixture over the noodles. Sprinkle with the remaining cilantro and serve at once.

shrimp sauce with lemon & herbs

very easy   serves 4

15–20 minutes   10 minutes

ingredients

12 oz/350 g dried spaghettini or vermicelli

4 tbsp olive oil

4 tbsp butter

8 scallions, green part included, sliced thinly

1 lb/450 g raw shrimp, shelled

juice and finely grated peel of ½ lemon

3 tbsp chopped fresh flatleaf parsley

3 tbsp shredded fresh basil

1 tbsp chopped fresh marjoram or oregano

2 tsp chopped fresh thyme

1 cup chicken bouillon

salt and pepper

Cook the pasta in plenty of boiling salted water until al dente. Drain and return to the pan and cover to keep warm.

Heat the oil and butter in a large skillet over a medium-high heat. Add the scallions and shrimp. Stir-fry for 2 minutes, or until the shrimp turn pink. Reduce the heat to medium. Stir in the lemon juice and peel, herbs, and chicken bouillon. Season with salt and pepper. Simmer until heated through.

Transfer the pasta to a warm serving dish. Pour the shrimp mixture over the pasta and toss well to mix. Serve at once.

scallops with porcini & cream sauce

very easy   serves 4

10 minutes +
20 minutes
soaking time   25 minutes

ingredients

1⅓ cups dried porcini mushrooms
generous 2 cups hot water
3 tbsp olive oil
3 tbsp butter
1½ cups scallops, sliced
2 garlic cloves, chopped very finely

2 tbsp lemon juice
1 cup heavy cream
salt and pepper
12 oz/350 g dried fettuccine or pappardelle
2 tbsp chopped fresh flatleaf parsley

Put the porcini and hot water in a bowl. Let soak for 20 minutes. Strain the mushrooms, reserving the soaking water, and chop coarsely. Line a strainer with paper towels and strain the mushroom water into a bowl.

Heat the oil and butter in a large skillet over a medium heat. Add the scallops and cook for 2 minutes, until just golden. Add the garlic and mushrooms, then stir-fry for another minute.

Stir in the lemon juice, cream, and ½ cup of the mushroom water. Bring to a boil, then simmer over a medium heat for 2–3 minutes, stirring constantly, until the liquid is reduced by half. Season with salt and pepper. Remove from the heat.

Cook the pasta in plenty of boiling salted water until al dente. Drain and transfer to a warm serving dish. Briefly reheat the sauce and pour over the pasta. Sprinkle with the parsley and toss well to mix. Serve at once.

tuna with garlic, lemon, capers & olives

extremely easy

serves 4

10 minutes

10 minutes

ingredients

3 cups dried conchiglie

4 tbsp olive oil

4 tbsp butter

3 large garlic cloves, sliced thinly

7 oz/200 g canned tuna, drained
  and broken into chunks

2 tbsp lemon juice

1 tbsp capers, drained

10–12 black olives, pitted and sliced

2 tbsp chopped fresh flatleaf parsley

Cook the pasta in plenty of boiling salted water until al dente. Drain and return to the pan.

Heat the olive oil and half the butter in a skillet over a medium-low heat. Add the garlic and cook for a few seconds, until just beginning to color. Reduce the heat to low. Add the tuna, lemon juice, capers, and olives. Stir gently until all the ingredients are heated through.

Transfer the pasta to a warm serving dish. Pour the tuna mixture over the pasta. Add the parsley and remaining butter. Toss well to mix. Serve at once.

mussels with tomatoes, bell peppers & olives

very easy

serves 4

20 minutes 20 minutes

12½ cups mussels
1 large onion, chopped finely
1 cup dry white wine
3 tbsp olive oil
3 garlic cloves, chopped very finely
2 yellow bell peppers, seeded and diced

14 oz/400 g canned chopped tomatoes
¼ tsp dried chili flakes
salt and pepper
1 lb/450 g riccioli or fettucine
10–12 black olives, pitted and sliced
6 tbsp shredded fresh basil

Clean the mussels by scrubbing the shells and pulling out any beards that are attached. Rinse well and discard any with broken shells and any that do not close when tapped. Put the mussels in a large pan with the onion and white wine. Cover and cook over a medium heat for 3–4 minutes, shaking the pan, until the mussels open. Remove from the heat. Lift out the mussels with a perforated spoon, reserving the liquid. Discard any that remain closed. Remove the rest of the mussels from their shells.

Heat the olive oil and garlic in a skillet over a medium-low heat. Cook until the garlic is just beginning to color. Add the bell peppers, tomatoes, chili flakes and 4 tablespoons of the mussel liquid. Bring to a boil, then simmer over a medium heat for 15 minutes, or until slightly reduced. Season with salt and pepper. Cook the pasta until al dente. Drain and transfer to a serving dish. Add the mussels and olives to the sauce; stir until heated. Pour onto the pasta. Add the basil and mix well. Serve at once.

mussels with white wine, garlic & parsley

ingredients

very easy   serves 4

20 minutes   10 minutes

14 cups mussels
1 large onion, chopped
3 garlic cloves, chopped very finely
generous 2 cups dry white wine
1 bay leaf
2 sprigs of fresh thyme

5 tbsp chopped fresh flatleaf parsley
1 tbsp chopped fresh rosemary
4 tbsp butter
salt and pepper
1 lb/450 g dried tagliatelle or other
   broad-ribboned pasta

Clean the mussels by scrubbing the shells and pulling out any beards that are attached. Rinse well, discarding any with broken shells or that remain open when tapped. Put the onion, garlic, white wine, herbs, and 2 tablespoons of the butter in a pan. Bring to a boil, then reduce the heat. Add the mussels. Season to taste. Cover and cook over a medium heat for 3–4 minutes, shaking the pan, until the mussels open. Remove from the heat. Lift out the mussels with a perforated spoon, reserving the liquid. Discard any that remain closed. Remove most of the others from their shells, reserving a few in their shells to garnish.

Cook the pasta until al dente. Drain and put the pasta into bowls. Spoon the mussels over the pasta. Strain the mussel liquid and return to the pan. Add the remaining butter and heat until melted. Pour over the pasta, then garnish with the mussels in their shells and serve at once.

smoked salmon, sour cream & mustard sauce

extremely easy · serves 4

10 minutes · 10 minutes

ingredients

1 lb/450 g tagliatelle or conchiglie
1¼ cups sour cream
2 tsp Dijon mustard
4 large scallions, sliced finely
8 oz/225 g smoked salmon,
 cut into bite-size pieces

finely grated peel of ½ lemon
pepper

2 tbsp chopped fresh chives, to garnish

Cook the pasta in plenty of boiling salted water until al dente. Drain and return to the pan. Add the sour cream, mustard, scallions, smoked salmon, and lemon peel to the pasta. Stir over a low heat until heated through. Season with pepper.

Transfer to a serving dish. Sprinkle with the chives. Serve warm or at room temperature.

hot cajun seafood sauce

very easy   serves 4

15 minutes   20 minutes

ingredients

generous 2 cups whipping cream

8 scallions, sliced thinly

scant 1 cup chopped fresh flatleaf parsley

1 tbsp chopped fresh thyme

½ tbsp freshly ground black pepper

½–1 tsp dried chili flakes

1 tsp salt

1 lb/450 g dried fusilli or tagliatelle

scant ½ cup freshly grated Gruyère cheese

scant ¼ cup freshly grated Parmesan cheese

2 tbsp olive oil

8 oz/225 g raw shrimp, shelled

1 cup scallops, sliced

1 tbsp shredded fresh basil, to garnish

Heat the cream in a large pan over a medium heat, stirring constantly. When almost boiling, reduce the heat and add the scallions, parsley, thyme, pepper, chili flakes, and salt. Simmer for 7–8 minutes, stirring, until thickened. Remove from the heat.

Cook the pasta in plenty of boiling salted water until al dente. Drain and return to the pan. Add the cream mixture and the cheeses to the pasta. Toss over a low heat until the cheeses have melted. Transfer to a warm serving dish.

Heat the oil in a large skillet over a medium-high heat. Add the shrimp and scallops. Stir-fry for 2–3 minutes, until the shrimp have just turned pink.

Pour the seafood over the pasta and toss well to mix. Sprinkle with the basil. Serve at once.

index